Serim Publishing

**Essay Writing Step-by-Step**

Published by Serim Publishing Co.
Registration: 6-792
Address: 504, Jungil Bldg 349-6 Gil-dong, Gangdong-gu, Seoul, Korea<134-010>
Phone: +82-2-488-3280
Fax: +82-2-488-3281

First Published 2008.1.5
Written by Young Woo Park
Edited by Jeffrey Zhang, Jay Lee, Sean Mahoney
Adviced by Yang Soo Lim/ President of Incheon Elementary Teacher's Association

Price ₩12,000
ISBN 978-89-92576-15-4 13740

## How to write My Essay better?

Today, we are faced with a lot of situations where we must write an essay. We are writing English essays for various purposes in our lives such as taking several kinds of exams for entrance to special high schools and universities, applying for work, and also for our own personal needs. However, we are left wondering if our essays are good enough for these purposes. Now, it has become necessary to develop skills in writing a good essay. We must learn to form ideas and then express them to others in an organized, well developed, and clear manner. Writing is the most powerful forms of communication and an essential skill of language.

This book is based on way to improve the students' writing skills and develop their way of thinking. Through this book, I hope all the students will succeed in their school achievements and further purposes.

*Young Woo Park*

# Contents

## Unit 1 How to Think



## Unit 2 Composing Topics



## Unit 3 How to Develop the Idea

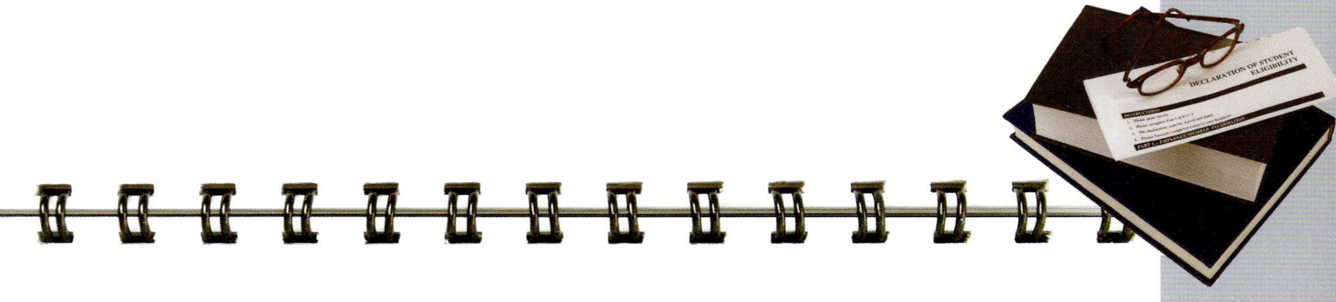

Contents

## Unit 4 Introduction and Body of an Essay



## Unit 5 Conclusion



## Unit 6 Information for Essays

# Unit 1

# How to Think

## Introduction

When we look at a beautiful painting, we think it is beautiful. However, sometimes it is difficult to say why it is beautiful. Similarly, when we read a good essay, we like it, but it is difficult to say why. If we understand the message and it gives us new knowledge, emotion or feeling, it is a good essay.
In order to think more logically and creatively, try to do the following.

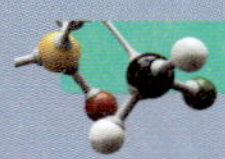

## Seven steps to aid in the thought process

1. Look at and think of the object carefully
2. Use your full imagination
3. Try to be flexible
4. Be open-minded
5. Make your ideas clear and well organized
6. Don't hesitate to make your own composition
7. Focus on your idea till the end of your essay

## Brain storming

Brain storming is a way of thinking of ideas. We can think of a topic and try to write as many words as we can be related to the picture. Then, we can use the words to make sentences. Write down anything that comes to your mind. Here we will look at pictures to get the topic and help us think.

# Lesson 1 A Rose

**A** What words or ideas can you get from this flower?

| One word | | |
|---|---|---|
| | | |
| | | |
| | | |
| | | |

| Two or more words | |
|---|---|
| | |
| | |
| | |
| | |

**B** Now, use your words to make 5 sentences about the flower.

**C** If you have this flower, what would you want to do with it?

Teacher's comment

# Lesson 2 Computers





A What ideas and words can you get from this picture?

One word

Two or more words

B Now, use your words to make 5 sentences about computers.

C Do you think computers help us? Why or Why not?

Teacher's comment

# Lesson 3 Country Life



**A** What ideas and words can you get from this picture?

| One word | | |
|---|---|---|
| | | |
| | | |
| | | |
| | | |

| Two or more words | |
|---|---|
| | |
| | |
| | |
| | |

**B** Now, use your words to make 5 sentences about country life.

**C** Would you like to live in the country? Why or Why not?

**Teacher's comment**

# Lesson 4 Seaside Memories

What ideas and words can you get from this picture?

**One word**

**Two or more words**

**B** Now, use your words to make 5 sentences about the seaside.

**C** Write about a seaside memory you have.

Teacher's comment

# Lesson 5 Family Picnic

**A** What ideas and words can you get from this picture?

| One word | | |
|---|---|---|
| | | |
| | | |
| | | |
| | | |

| Two or more words | |
|---|---|
| | |
| | |
| | |
| | |

B Now, use your words to make 5 sentences about family activities.

C What do you like to do with your family? Why?

Teacher's comment

# Unit 2 Composing Topics

Before you start writing an essay, you will have a topic. Sometimes the topic is given to you, but other times you must think of it yourself. Here, we will practice thinking of a topic before writing.

## Introduction

Most essays have a purpose or goal. It can be to teach us about a topic, for example, an essay about "the internet." This essay would introduce the topic of the internet and give us information about it. Also, an essay can be about an idea or an opinion, for example, "smoking is bad." This essay would give reasons why smoking is bad for us. An essay can be about anything, but a good essay makes us think about the topic.

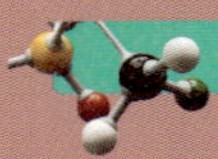

## A good essay usually has one or more of these points.

- Originality (it is not the same as other essays)
- Enthusiasm (your essay must be interesting and have energy)
- A new way of looking at old views (new ideas)
- Clear and well-developed (good sentences and well organized essay form)

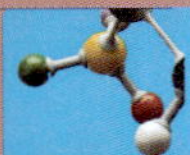

## The opposite of these characteristics is easy to see. A bad essay

- Restates views already stated elsewhere (the same as other essays)
- Overly simplistic vocabulary (the words are too easy)
- Is unclear, unorganized, or boring (bad sentences and organization)
- Contains a lot of filler information and padding that is of little consequence to the argument (information not about the topic)

# Lesson 1 Topic 1

In recent years, the number of youngsters eating out rather than having home-cooked meals has risen considerably. Many claim that this is due to the fact that family members now have very separate lifestyles, so youngsters often have to take care of themselves and choose the quickest solution.

Read the above story carefully and try to find out the topic. Remember the topic is only one or a few words. Also, compose a topic sentence yourself.

Topic word(s) :

Topic sentence :

## B Write your own story according to the topic.

## C After correcting your writing, rewrite.

Teacher's comment

Lesson 2

# Topic 2

In the past, people tended to shop at small, local, family businesses. There, they would be sure to have welcome smiles and some local gossip as they spent half an hour doing their daily shopping. As time passed and more and more women spent longer hours in the workplace, methods of shopping also changed.

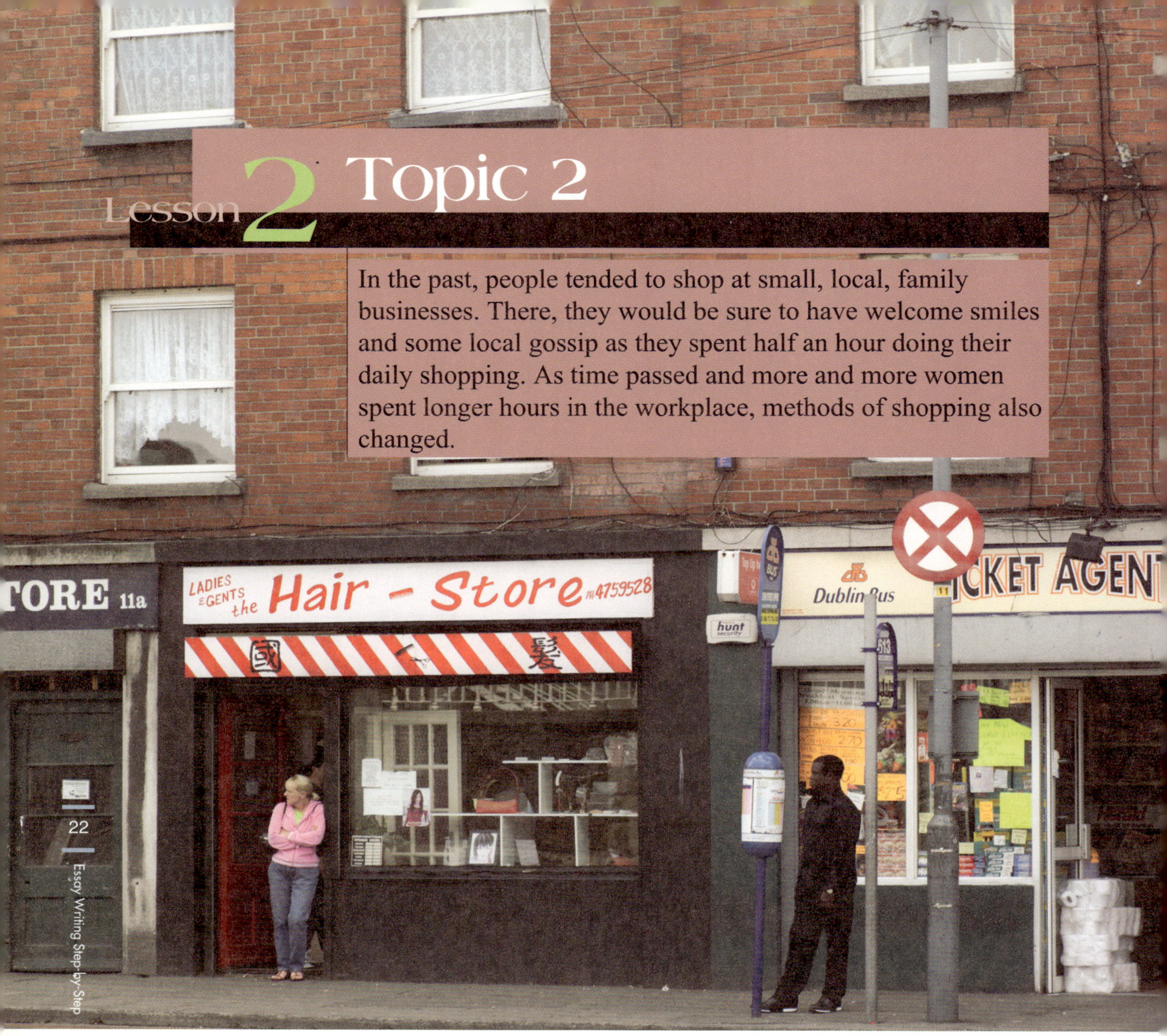

Read the above story carefully and try to find out the topic. Remember the topic is only one or a few words. Also, compose a topic sentence yourself.

Topic word(s) : ______________________

Topic sentence : ______________________

______________________

______________________

B Write your own story according to the topic.

C After correcting your writing, rewrite.

Teacher's comment

# Lesson 3 Topic 3

I graduated from Korea University last year eith a degree in English education and have been working at an ESL school since October. I will be free during the holidays, from the end of June until the beginning of October. I would love a job teaching English with teenagers at your camp. I am a friendly, happy person who works alone and in a team. I think I am hardworking, highly energetic and also enjoy working with kids a lot. English is the world language and L believe students everywhere in the world should have a chane to study it. I think a camp is a perfect way to learn and practice English. I hope I can join your camp and help you make it great.

Yours faithfully,
Joe Smith

Read the above story carefully and try to find out the topic. Remember the topic is only one or a few words. Also, compose a topic sentence yourself.

Topic word(s) : ____________________

Topic sentence : ____________________

If you wanted to work at a Summer English Camp, you would need to write your application with a cover letter. Write your own cover letter for applying for this job. Look at the given advertisement below.

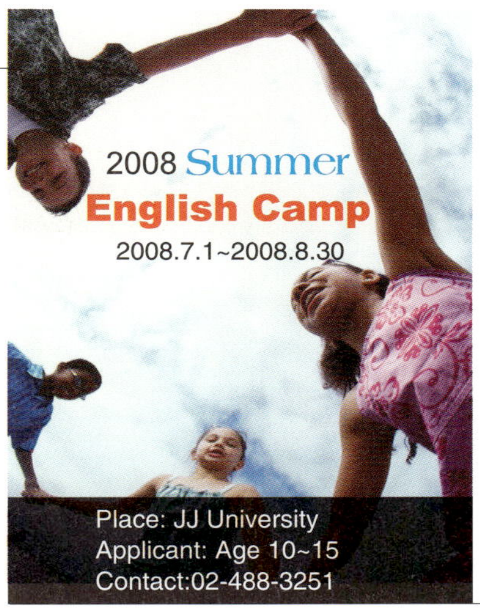


B Write your cover letter.

# Lesson 4 Topic 4

I wake up everyday and go to my job at the resaurnat. I'm a waitress at a small restaurant in our town. I really enjoy my job and I love our customers. When I serve them delicious food. it makes them happy. That me happy, too. Our diner is busy for breakfast, lunch and dinner. Everyone in town comes here to eat. Our menu has a lot of home-style favorites such as a hamburger and or bacon and eggs. I like to talk to the people who come to eat listen to them as they talk about their lives. Being a waitress can be hard, but it's the perfect job for me! Especially when I get a big tip!

Read the above story carefully and try to find out the topic. Remember the topic is only one or a few words. Also, compose a topic sentence yourself.

Topic word(s) : ______

Topic sentence : ______

B Write your own story according to the topic.

C After correcting your writing, rewrite.

Teacher's comment

# Lesson 5 Topic 5

As a child I hated sports and I'd have done anything to get out of PE. That all changed when I had a baby. I put on quite a bit of weight, so I went to a gym to get back into shape. Soon I was hooked and I was going everyday and doing aerobics, too. I lost weight and my body became very toned. Then, when the gym expanded, my aerobics instructor asked if I had thought about becoming an instructor myself and why I didn't get qualified so I could take over some of the extra classes. I decided to do it and I haven't looked back since. Now, I love my job. I get a great feeling seeing my students get slim and fit. I've made a lot of friends and my self-confidence has improved, too.

Read the above story carefully and try to find out the topic. Remember the topic is only one or a few words. Also compose a topic sentence yourself.

Topic word(s) : ______

Topic sentence : ______

B Write your own story according to the topic.

C After correcting your writing, rewrite.

Teacher's comment

# Unit 3 How to Develop the Idea

What makes an essay great? The answer is easy: A great essay makes the reader think about the topic. Of course a good essay will be well-written and organized. However, more importantly, it will be interesting. It can make you angry, happy or sad, but it will always hold the readers attention. A good essay will make you think, feel, and understand new things.

*To make your essay easy and interesting, you need to try to set your idea first and then feel free to write about it. You can write about your ideas, feelings, memories or opinions. You can even give the reader information on the topic or write a story about the topic. You can write in many ways, but try to make it original and special.

## Seven Steps for Writing

1. Write about your idea freely
2. Organize your sentences logically, so your ideas are clear
3. Try to discuss your writing with your friends
4. Don't hesitate to correct any errors
5. Review and rewrite your essay
6. Be patient
7. Follow the rules of essay form and the writing process.

## The paragraph

An essay is made of paragraphs. Each paragraph is a group of sentences which all focus on one idea or purpose. In an essay, you can see the location of paragraphs as they are separated by empty lines. Remember each paragraph is about ONE idea or has ONE purpose.

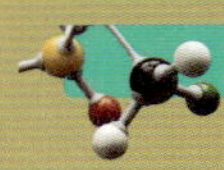

## The process of paragraph writing is this

words → sentences → paragraph

For example:

Words : love, flowers, hate, happy, beautiful, etc.

Sentences : Love means never to say sorry.
I love to give some flowers to my best friend.
Everybody likes to get some presents on his birthday.

## Paragraph Ⅰ : First impression

When I meet new people, I want to give them a good first impression. We want to send them smiles and talk to them with kindness. If I get a good impression from him, I will want to have another chance to meet them again. I might prepare for some flowers to give the person who he will meet for a second time, especially if the other person is a beautiful girl or lady.

Lesson 1

# Train Trip

## What does this picture make you think about?

Take some time and talk about this picture with your teacher and classmates.

Write down the sentences and ideas you think of with your class.

1. ______________________

______________________

2. ______________________

______________________

3. ______________________

______________________

4. ______________________

______________________

5. ______________________

B If you want to go on a trip by train, where do you want to go and with whom? Also what do you want to do when you get there?

Teacher's comment

# Lesson 2 Dating

Look at and think about this picture and take some time to discuss it with your teacher and classmates.

**A** Write down the sentences and ideas you think of with your class.

1. 

2. 

3. 

4. 

5. 

**B** If you have a chance to enjoy a date with your best girl(boy) friend, what do you want to prepare for the date and what will you do with your friend?

Teacher's comment

# Lesson 3 My Future Job

Take a look at this picture and then take some time to discuss it with your teacher and classmates.



**A** Write down the sentences and ideas you think of with your class.

1.

2.

3.

4.

5.

B What do you want to be in your future?

C Tell me the reason why you want to have this job.

D What do you need to study and prepare for this job?

E When and how can you achieve your goal?

# Lesson 4 Sports

Look over this picture and discuss it with your class and teacher.

Write down the sentences and ideas you think of with your class.

1.

2.

3.

4.

5.

**B** To be an athlete, one should train hard for a long time.
If you want to be an athlete, which sport will you choose?

## Teacher's comment

# Lesson 5 Difficult Job

Look over this picture and discuss it with your class and teacher.

Write down the sentences and ideas you think of with your class.

1.

2.

3.

4.

5.

B What kind of job do you think is difficult, dangerous, or dirty? Why? (Choose 3 jobs)

Teacher's comment

# Unit 4

# Introduction and Body of an Essay

## Introduction

To be a good essay, it must have a good introduction. The introduction is the first paragraph of an essay. In the introduction the topic of the essay is introduced. The first sentence of the introduction usually tells us the topic, this is called the "topic sentence." After the topic sentence, background information about the topic is given to the reader. Then the main idea of the essay is introduced. The "main idea" is the idea that you will talk about in the essay.

A good essay has a good body.
The body in a short essay usually has 2 or 3 paragraphs. Each paragraph in the body has a supporting idea that helps explain the main idea. We use reasons, examples, facts, personal experiences, and so on to support the main idea in the body.

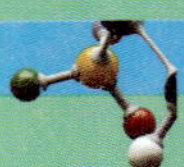

## Steps for writing an introduction and body

- set your topic
- get your main idea
- build your introduction with background information

Lesson 1

# Getting Main Idea and Background Information

## Practice 1 Main Idea

Think of three main ideas for each of these topics

### A Dog

ex Dogs are man's best friend.

1. 
2. 
3. 

### B School

ex There should be no school on Saturday.

1. 
2. 
3. 

## Food

ex There are many good and bad things about fast food.

1. ______________________________

2. ______________________________

3. ______________________________

## Teacher

ex Teachers are very kind and teach a lot of things to students.

1. ______________________________

2. ______________________________

3. ______________________________

## Background Information

The introduction gives us background information about a topic. For example, if the topic is "Cars," we can think of background information about cars such as:

- Cars are the most popular and comfortable form of transportation in the world.
- In many countries, almost every family has at least one car, sometimes two or three.
- The first car was made in 1769, in Paris.
- The number of car accidents is rapidly increasing.
- So many people have been killed by car accidents.

Write three examples of background information for these topics.

### A Bears

ex Bears sleep during the winter.

1. ______________________________

2. ______________________________

3. ______________________________

## B Earth

ex Earth has many kinds of life such as animals, plants and humans.

1. ______________________________

2. ______________________________

3. ______________________________

## C Soccer

ex Soccer is a team sport, played on a grass field or pitch.

1. ______________________________

2. ______________________________

3. ______________________________

# Lesson 2 Writing the Introduction

Look at the these examples of introduction paragraphs. Look for the main idea and the background information. The topic sentence introduces the topic.

**Example 1**

Sports are an important and healthy part of all students' lives. Of course, sports can be important in everyone's life, but sports are especially important to students. This is because sports can affect students in ways that will help them for the rest of their lives. Parents and schools should encourage children to play sports for all of the benefits that sports provide. There are a lot of reasons why sports can benefit a student.

**Example 2**

Fast food is becoming a major problem in today's society. It is easy to see that fast food is becoming more and more popular all the time. Fast food restaurants are continuously being made in everyone's neighborhood. With so many fast food restaurants being built, it is easier for people to buy fast food instead of cooking meals at home. Hence, the amount of people eating fast food increases every day. This increase of people eating fast food is causing many different problems in our world.

**Example 3**

The environment is our home. It is everything in nature around us. The actions of humans have changed the environment in very serious and dangerous ways. In order for people to stop damaging the environment, they need to become aware of how essential the environment is in our lives.

Now discuss these topics with your class and teacher.
Then write a topic sentence and background information.

## Example 1

Topic Sentence:

Background Information:

## Example 2

Topic Sentence:

Background Information:

## Example 3

Topic Sentence:

Background Information:

# Lesson 3 Writing the Body

In the body, each paragraph is about one supporting idea. When you write a supporting idea, you may use the other's opinion or some date of a research. Also you can get some background information from various books.

For example, if the main idea is: "Smoking is bad for our health", the supporting ideas can be:

1. Cigarettes have many bad things in them.
2. Second hand smoke is bad for us, too.
3. Smoking kills many people.

Now try to write a few more supporting ideas for this topic.

4. ____________________
5. ____________________
6. ____________________
7. ____________________

- Topic : Church
- Main idea : Many churches help the poor.
- Supporting idea in the first paragraph :

- Supporting idea in the second paragraph

## Practice

Write as many supporting ideas as you can for each of these main ideas.

**A** A good friend is very important.

ex A good friend helps you when you have a problem.

- Supporting idea in the first paragraph :

- Supporting idea in the second paragraph

B Everyone should have a hobby.

ex Hobbies are a good way to have fun.

- Supporting idea in the first paragraph :

- Supporting idea in the second paragraph

C America is a very strong country.

ex American has many big companies, such as Coke and Nike.

- Supporting idea in the first paragraph :

- Supporting idea in the second paragraph

## D Studying English is important.

ex English is the world language.

- Supporting idea in the first paragraph :

- Supporting idea in the second paragraph

## E New technology will continue to make our lives easier.

ex Multiple technologies are being combined into one machine, such as in cell phones.

- Supporting idea in the first paragraph :

- Supporting idea in the second paragraph

# Lesson 4 Examples of the Body

Now take a look at these examples of an essay body written by students. Look for the supporting idea in each paragraph. Try to guess what the main idea is. Looking at body examples written by students will help you to develop your own essay. After reading the following essay examples carefully, try to set your mind on how to make your essay better.

### Body Paragraph 1

First, sports are good for students because it is excellent exercise. To have good health, it is necessary for students to exercise often. Playing sports such as soccer, basketball, baseball are excellent ways for students to be healthy. These days students must study very hard to succeed in life. Regular exercise will help them have a healthy body and healthy mind.

### Body Paragraph 2

Second, sports help students learn about working together. Team sports require students to cooperate. Learning cooperation is an important skill for life. In a company, just like a sports team, people must work together. We must learn to help each other to achieve a goal. Playing sports can help students be ready for the future.

1. What is the topic of the above essay?

______________________________

2. Find all the supporting ideas of this essay.

______________________________

______________________________

______________________________

3. What do you think is the main idea of this essay?

______________________________

______________________________

______________________________

______________________________

**Body Paragraph 1**

To begin, fast food, which includes such foods as pizza and hamburgers, contains fats that have been shown to cause high cholesterol levels in many people. High cholesterol can be a major health risk and can lead to such health problems as strokes and heart attacks. Furthermore, it is obvious that fast food causes many people to be overweight. Carrying too much extra body fat is also a serious health risk. Thus, fast food can be harmful to one's health.

**Body Paragraph 2**

The second negative effect of fast food is that it shortens the amount of time families spend together. Dining together as a family creates much needed social time for a family. It allows a family time to interact with each other. However, fast food meals are replacing regular family meals. A fast food meal does not provide the same amount of time for families to spend together. In fact, the time is a lot shorter. Therefore, fast food makes relationships among family members weaker than regular meals do.



1. What is the topic of the above essay?

______________________________

2. Find all the supporting ideas of this essay.

______________________________

______________________________

______________________________

3. What do you think is the main idea of this essay?

______________________________

______________________________

______________________________

______________________________

### Body Paragraph 1

One reason why the environment is so important is because of our health. The air we breathe, the water we drink, even the food we eat, all come from nature. So, if nature is polluted and unhealthy, then, of course, everything we put into our bodies will also be unhealthy. Therefore, if our natural environment is damaged, then our health will also be damaged. The environment should be protected to make sure that people continue to be healthy.

### Body Paragraph 2

Another important issue about the environment is renewable resources, such as wood and clothing material. If we keep damaging our environment, then things that we use every day will become less and less. We need to stop destroying forests, so we can continue to use the resources found in those places. These resources are very important to our way of life.

1. What is the topic of the above essay?

___

2. Find all the supporting ideas of this essay.

___

___

___

3. What do you think is the main idea of this essay?

___

___

___

___

# Lesson 5 Writing Practice for the Body





Now try to write two body paragraphs for each of these main ideas. Look at the examples in lesson 4. Each body paragraph should have a supporting idea and then information, examples, or reasons to develop the supporting idea.

**Main idea** Korea is a great country.

1. Korean food is healthy and delicious.

2. Korean people are kind.

**Main idea** Everyone needs money.

1. We need money to live.

2. We need money to have fun.

**Main idea** Being a good student is difficult.

1. Students have to study very, very much.

2. Parents really want us to get good scores at school.

Now try to think of your own topic and main idea. Remember the "Supporting Idea" is the first sentence of each body paragraph.

**Main idea**

1.

2.

# Unit 5

# Conclusion

## Introduction

A good essay has a reasonable conclusion. The conclusion is very important. It is like the end of a movie or book. It must be interesting and make us think more. Also, it must finish the essay strongly and clearly. You can write a summary of your ideas from the introduction and body and introduce concluding ideas that make us think more about the topic.

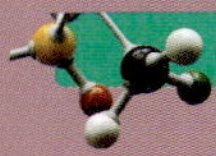

## In the conclusion, you can write:

1. A summary of the main idea and supporting ideas in new and different sentences.
2. Also the last sentence of the conclusion is very important. It is called the "concluding sentence". It is usually similar to the main idea. The concluding sentence should finish the essay in a thought provoking way.

# Lesson 1 Paraphrasing

Paraphrasing is writing sentences in your own words: changing the words and forms to make a new sentence with the same meaning. This is helpful when writing a summary. In this part the writer should keep in mind that the main idea and supporting idea should not be changed.

## Practice 1

Try paraphrasing these sentences.

ex Reading is a good way to learn about many topics.
Books can give us information on a large number of subjects.

1. There are many fun outdoor activities that are popular in summer.

2. Becoming a doctor is the dream of many young students.

3. Playing computer games too much can be bad for you.

4. The internet can help students study in many ways.

5. Traveling is a great way to learn about the world.

## Practice 2

Read these short paragraphs and then write a summary in your own words (paraphrasing).

1. Are animals happy in a zoo? The zoo keepers give them food, clean them, help them when they are sick and are always very kind to them. Many people can come to see the animals and learn many things about them. The problem with animals in a zoo is that they are not free.

2. Eating breakfast is very important for everyone. In the morning we need a lot of energy to study or work during the day. In America most people like to eat toast, eggs, ham and maybe some fruit. A good drink to have is milk or orange juice.

# Lesson 2 Concluding Sentences

Write a concluding sentence for each of these conclusion samples. The concluding sentence should paraphrase the main idea in a new and interesting way.

1. In conclusion, vacations are important for students. It gives them a chance to relax and relieve their stress. Also, it is a good time for extra studies in areas such as sports, language or music.

   **concluding sentence**

2. To sum up, cars are a huge problem for the environment. They release dangerous chemicals into the air. These chemicals make the air polluted and cause global warming.

   **concluding sentence**

Teacher's comment

3. All things considered, it must be said that computers are important for our lives. When connected to the internet, they become a powerful tool for communication and information transfer. Also, a computer can do something that would take a person hours in only a few seconds.

**concluding sentence**

4. To conclude, a present is a wonderful thing to give to another person. A present can be a way to remember a special event like a birthday or wedding. Also, giving a present shows love and appreciation to a family member, friend, co-worker or class-mate.

**concluding sentence**

5. To summarize, robots will be helpful to us in the future. First, they can do dangerous jobs that people can't do. In addition, they can be stronger, smarter and better than people in many ways.

**concluding sentence**

6. In summary, spring is my favorite season. Spring represents the beginning of life. Baby animals and new flowers appear in spring. It is also a season for great weather. It is not too cold or too hot, but nice and warm.

**concluding sentence**

## Proverbs

### "A bird in the hand is worth two in the bush."

It is better to hold on to something which you already have, than to try to get something less attainable; you might not succeed in getting it and you might even risk losing what you have: Jack went for several interviews and has already been offered a job which he has either to accept or reject right away. He really has to decide whether a bird in the hand is worth two in the bush, because he is still waiting to hear about a job with much better prospects.

### "A burnt child dreads the fire"

A person who has a bad experience concerning something will avoid it in future: Jill says that she was so unhappy when she was married that she will never marry again; a burnt child dreads the fire, I suppose. Mary had such a bad time giving birth to her daughter that she is not going to have any more children. She may change her mind, but it could be the case that a burnt child dreads the fire. A burnt child dreads the fire and Sue's already had a bad experience from buying a second-hand car. This time she says that she's buying a brand-new one.

### "A cat may look at a king"

There is no reason why an ordinary or humble person should not look at someone of great importance. This proverb is used to emphasize equality of people and is often said when someone is accused of staring at someone else : 'Why are you staring at me?' the beautiful young woman asked the rather shabby young man on the bus. 'I wasn't staring,' he replied, 'and a cat may look at a king.' The child was looking in wonder at the jewels which the old lady was wearing. When the old lady pushed him aside haughtily, the child's mother said angrily, 'A cat may look at a king.'

# Lesson 3 Writing the Conclusion

Look at these examples of the conclusion, then write your own.

## conclusion 1 from Lesson 4 in Unit 4

To conclude, sports are good for students for many reasons. Some of the most important reasons are that sports make students healthier, and also teach them how to co-operate better. Being healthy and having good cooperation skills are two very important things for students to learn and to keep for the rest of their lives. Since students can gain both of these qualities from sports, they benefit students in very positive ways.

**Now write the conclusion in your way**

Teacher's comment

## conclusion 2 from Lesson 4 in Unit 4

To summarize, our natural environment is very important in many areas of life, including health and materials we use every day to survive. It is very easy to see that protecting the environment protects our health. Moreover, if we stop damaging our environment, we will continue to have resources that are very useful to us. It is for these reasons that people should realize how important the environment is in our lives.

**Now write the conclusion in your way**

## Teacher's comment

## How to Write Your Conclusion

In conclusion, the amount of fast food in our society is leading to many harmful effects among people. The negative effects of fast food impact two important areas in a person's life. These areas are health and social relationships. It is harmful to our health because of the amount of grease and fat contained in fast food. Also, it is harmful to social relationships because it decreases the amount of time a family spends together. The negative impacts of fast food on these two important areas of life prove that fast food is a serious problem in modern society.

### Explanation

"It is harmful to our health because of the amount of grease and fat contained in fast food." It should be noted that this sentence shows the supporting idea from body paragraph 1. Thus, each sentence in a conclusion should summarize the supporting idea of each body paragraph.

"It is harmful to social relationships because it decreases the amount of time a family spends together." You can see that this sentence summarizes the supporting idea from body paragraph 2.

It is very important to restate the supporting ideas from the body in the conclusion.

“This increase of people eating fast food is causing many different problems in our world.”

“The negative impacts of fast food on these two important areas of life prove that fast food is a serious problem in modern society.”

These two sentences, one taken from the introduction and the other taken from the conclusion, are very similar. In fact, they express the same idea: the main idea. The final sentences in both the introduction and conclusion should explain the main idea.

Hint: Looking at the final sentence of the introduction will help you to write a concluding sentence in your conclusion.

# Lesson 4 Parts of an Essay Review

Now look at these 2 example essays in full and answer each of the questions

## Essay 1

Sports are an important and healthy part of all students' lives. Of course, sports can be important in everyone's life, but sports are especially important to students. This is because sports can affect students in ways that will help them for the rest of their lives. Parents and schools should encourage children to play sports for all of the benefits that sports provide. There are a lot of reasons why sports can benefit a student.

First, sports are good for students because it is excellent exercise. To have good health, it is necessary for students to exercise often. Playing sports such as soccer, basketball, baseball are excellent ways for students to be healthy. These days students must study very hard to succeed in life. Regular exercise will help them have a healthy body and healthy mind.

Second, sports help students learn about working together. Team sports require students to cooperate. Learning cooperation is an important skill for life. In a company, just like a sports team, people must work together. We must learn to help each other to achieve a goal. Playing sports can help students be ready for the future.

To conclude, sports are good for students for many reasons. Some of the most important reasons are that sports make students healthier, and also teach them how to cooperate better. Being healthy and having good cooperation skills are two very important things for students to learn and to keep for the rest of their lives. Since students can gain both of these qualities from sports, they benefit students in very positive ways.

- What is the topic?

- Write the topic sentence.

- Write the background information.

- Write the main idea.

- Write supporting idea 1.

- Write supporting idea 2.

- Write the concluding sentence.

## Essay 2

Fast food is becoming a major problem in today's society. It is easy to see that fast food is becoming more and more popular all the time. Fast food restaurants are continuously being made in everyone's neighborhood. With so many fast food restaurants being built, it is easier for people to buy fast food instead of cooking meals at home. Hence, the amount of people eating fast food increases every day. This increase of people eating fast food is causing many different problems in our world.

To begin, fast food, which includes such foods as pizza and hamburgers, contains fats that have been shown to cause high cholesterol levels in many people. High cholesterol can be a major health risk and can lead to such health problems as strokes and heart attacks. Furthermore, it is obvious that fast food causes many people to be overweight. Carrying too much extra body fat is also a serious health risk. Thus, fast food can be harmful to one's health.

The second negative effect of fast food is that it shortens the amount of time families spend together. Dining together as a family creates much needed social time for a family. It allows a family time to interact with each other. However, fast food meals are replacing regular family meals. A fast food meal does not provide the same amount of time for families to spend together. In fact, the time is a lot shorter. Therefore, fast food makes relationships among family members weaker than regular meals do.

In conclusion, the amount of fast food in our society is leading to many harmful effects among people. The negative effects of fast food impact two important areas in a person's life. These areas are health and social relationships. It is harmful to our health because of the amount of grease and fat contained in fast food. Also, it is harmful to social relationships because it decreases the amount of time a family spends together. The negative impacts of fast food on these two important areas of life prove that fast food is a serious problem in modern society.

• What is the topic?

• Write the topic sentence.

• Write the background information.

• Write the main idea.

• Write supporting idea 1.

• Write supporting idea 2.

• Write the concluding sentence.

# Lesson 5 Write Your Own Essay

So far, we have learned about the parts of an essay: the introduction, body and conclusion. Now you will try to write your own essay.

First we must write a essay outline. An essay outline is a plan for your essay. If you make a outline for your essay before you write. It will make writing your essay much easier.

## An example of an essay outline.

- Topic Television
- Main Idea Television is helpful to students in many ways.
- Supporting Idea 1 Students can get much information from TV.
- Supporting Idea 2 Watching fun programs can help students relieve stress.



Write an outline for your essay.

- Topic

_______________

- Main Idea:

_______________

- Supporting idea 1

_______________

- Supporting Idea 2

_______________

Now, using your outline, write an essay including an introduction, body and conclusion.

Introduction

Body

Conclusion

Now show your essay to your teacher. Talk about mistakes and things that need to be changed. Listen to your teacher and try to make your essay better.

Write the final copy of the essay including all corrections and changes.

Introduction

Body

## Proverbs

### "Faith will move mountains"

This proverb emphasizes the power which faith, such as religious faith, or a fervent belief in something has"

The young woman was told by medical experts that she would never be able to have children, but she prayed every day and eventually, to the amazement of the doctors, became pregnant; faith will move mountains.

The old woman was said to be terminally ill with cancer, but she had tremendous faith in the powers of the complementary medicine specialist and she lived for several more years; faith will move mountains.

Bill's parents refused to believe that he was dead, although they were told by army officers that no soldier had survived the battle where he was last seen. However, faith will move mountains; several years later Bill was released by the enemy forces who had taken him captive during the battle.

### Conclusion

# Unit 6

# Information for Essays

We have a lot of opportunity to write essays for several purposes. When ever we start to write essay, we take time to choose the subject and compose the body. Useful reading materials are necessary for the students to prepare for their own essays. Some say that reading is leading. To make our essay better, we need to read as many books as possible in order to get much basic knowledge, on topics such as social affairs, education, politics and economics.

It is not easy to write a good essay without training. In this part we will get some basic information through reading the materials. After getting the information, try to write about your own idea on the given topic.

# Lesson 1 Economics

## 1. How the Economy Grows

Four main things are needed for a country to make goods and services. These things, are called, natural resources, capital, labor force, and technology. Natural resources are all land, trees, water, sunlight and so on. Capital is all factories, tools, supplies, and equipment. Capital also means "money." Labor force means all the people who work or are looking for work. Technology means science and business ideas.

To be strong a country, it must use its natural resources to make factories, equipment, and other capital. This capital can make more goods in the future. A country must make many things to sell, such as food and clothing. Also a country must have scientists, workers, and business managers who will be leaders in the future.

In a strong country with a strong economy, saving and investment is also very important. When people save a lot of money, they use it to buy useful things like factories and machines. People who save money put money in the bank. The bank can lend money to people who want to start a company. If many people invest in companies, they will grow and the economy will grow.

What things do you think are the most important in our country to develop the economy?

## 2. World Trade

Almost everyone agrees that countries benefit from trading with one another. Everything country has different resources. For example, Canada has many trees and Saudi Arabia has much oil. Countries must trade to get the things they need. Every country should make goods that are easy for them to make and trade them for other resources they need. One country can't make everything. Countries must work together, so that we can all have the goods and resources we need to live. Some countries are afraid to share with other countries because they think if there is a war, trade will stop.

Some people say that we should not buy things from other countries, but try to build these things ourselves. They think that if they don't need to trade with other countries, their country will become strong and independent. One example of a country that doesn't want to trade with other countries is North Korea.

There are two ways a country can stop trading: tariffs, and import quotas. A tariff is a tax. It makes goods from foreign countries too expensive, so people don't want to buy them. An import quota is a limit for goods that come from foreign countries. For example, an import quota might say that only 10,000 cars from America can come to Korea in one year.

Do you think world trade is good for Korea? Give reasons for your answer.

# Lesson 2 Politics

## Government of the United States

### 1. Separation of Powers

In the United States the power of the government is divided into executive, legislative, and judicial parts. This is called the separation of powers. The executive part is the leaders of government, for example the President. The legislative part is the Congress. They make the laws for the country. The judicial part is the courts who protect the law. For example a judge would be in the judicial part. Each part works alone, but helps each other to govern the country. Each part of the government also makes sure the others parts are doing a good job. The President can "veto" laws, meaning that he can say a law made by the Congress is not good. Also, the President can choose who becomes a judge. The congress can make laws to control the leaders and the courts. The courts can decide if the Congress and President are doing something wrong. The parts of government in the United States work together to make a great country, but also watch each other and make sure everyone is doing the right thing.

What job in the government do you want to have? Why?

## 2. Political Parties and Election

The American people have a strong role in their government. They can join and help political parties. The United States has two major political parties, the Democratic and the Republican. Many people and groups help both of these parties all over the country. Members of these two parties are leaders of the United States government, including the President. This is called the two-party system, or bipartisan system.

There are also small political parties. Members of the small parties usually never become leaders of government. They sometimes talk about and work on problems the two major parties don't look at.

Elections are when the people can vote and choose who the leaders for the country will be. National elections to elect a President and Vice-President are held every four years on the first Tuesday in November. All members of the House of Representatives and about one-third of the members of the Senate are elected at this same time. Between the presidential elections, all of the representatives and another one-third or the senators are elected. This election is held on the same day in November every two years.

What changes would you make if you were the President of Korea?

# Lesson 3 Education

## 1. The Importance and Goal of Education.

Education is important because it helps people succeed in life. It gives people knowledge and understanding of the world. It helps them get skills such as playing sports, painting a picture, or playing a musical instrument. Education is an important part of everyone's life.

Education also helps people to change. These days, the world changes so quickly. We must always study to learn about these changes. For example, these days everyone must learn how to use the internet because it is needed for work, study and play.

There are three kinds of education: the psychomotor area, the cognitive area, and the affective area. The psychomotor area teaches skills using the body. Some of these skills are handwriting, speech, and physical education. They may be as easy as learning to use crayons or as difficult as learning ballet. In the cognitive area a person develops their knowledge and thinking. This is the largest area of education. When students study math problems, learn about history, read a novel, or practice a language, they are studying in the cognitive area. The affective area deals with feelings and values. It teaches students to be kind to others and also what is right and wrong in the world.

Which area of education do you think is the most important?

## 2. Kinds of Education

The school systems of all modern nations provide both general education and vocational education.

(1) General education General Education is the main focus of the school system from kindergarten to high school. Students study all the subjects of a complete education. General Education teaches students the basic knowledge that every person needs to know.

Almost all elementary education is general education. In every country, elementary school students are taught skills they will use in life such as reading, writing, and math. They also study other subjects, including geography, history, and science. After students finish elementary school, they usually move on to middle school or high school.

In middle and high school, students continue to study subjects such as social studies, mathematics, biology, physics, chemistry and languages. Tests become more important and students prepare to enter college or university. In Western countries, students also spend much time learning problem solving. They learn how to think of ways to solve problems we face in life.

(2) Vocational education - Vocational education helps students be ready for a job. Some high schools, called vocational high schools, specialize in vocational programs. Technical high schools are vocational high schools that teach students skills for jobs in technology, such as car repair, computers, and electronics. Vocational high school students also take some general educational courses. Universities and Colleges prepare students for jobs in architecture, business, engineering, law, medicine, nursing, pharmacy, teaching and so on.

Which Kind of education do you think is the most interesting?

# Lesson 4 History of the World

## 1. History of the World

The history of the world is the story of humans, from the first civilization to the space age. The story is about 5,000 years long, starting at about 3000 B.C. At that time, people made writing. When people started to write they could keep a diary of what happened in their lives. Today we study all the writings and these writings make up what we know as "World History." The time before writing started is called Prehistoric Times and the time after writing started is called Historic Times. There are four parts of Historic Times: Ancient Times, the Middle Ages, the early period of Modern Times, and Modern Times.

### Modern Times (the 1900's)

The 1900's were a time of great change. The thinking of people changed quickly. There were big and horrible wars. Governments were made and broken. Also, great discoveries in science and technology changed the world we live in. We even left Earth and explored Space.

In the early 1900's, much of world was controlled by strong European countries such as England. Soon, almost all of the world was free. Countries in Asia, Africa and South America became stronger. Also, the United States became a world super power. New technology made the world an exciting place. Things like airplanes, atomic energy, computers, refrigerators, televisions, plastic, and highways crowded with cars became a normal part of life.

The space age opened in 1957 when Russia launched the first satellite to circle the earth. In 1968, three American astronauts traveled around the moon. The following year, two American astronauts landed on the moon. Nowadays, science and technology keep growing faster and faster. Where will we be in 100, 200 or 300 years?

What do you think has been the greatest invention in Modern times? Give reasons and examples to support your answers.



## Proverbs

### "When in Rome, do as the Romans do"

When you are in another country or somewhere where people have different customs from you or behave differently from you, you should copy their manners, customs, etc. Women here cover their heads when they go to church and you should do the same; when in Rome, do as the Romans do. It's the custom there for dinner guests to arrive exactly on time and so we mustn't do what we would do in Britain and arrive about 15 minutes late; when in Rome, do as the Romans do. I have been living in southern Spain for a few months and now take a siesta in the middle of the day. It's a case of when in Rome, do as the Romans do, and it is a custom I very much approve of.

# Lesson 5 Literature

## 1. What is Literature?

Literature is everything that has ever been written. It includes comic books and magazines, as well as the novels of Mark Twain and the plays of William Shakespeare.

There are many kinds of literature. For example, we may read literature written in a kind of language. such as French literature. We also study writings about a group of people such as the literature of the American Indian. Literature can be from a time such as literature of the 1800's. We also read literature of a subject such as in the literature of animals.

Literature can be any writing, but usually when we say, "literature," we mean great pieces of writing. For example the novel, "Oliver Twist," written by Charles Dickens is literature, but a comic book a young student might read is not true literature. True literature is a valuable and treasured piece of writing, only the best writers can say they have written something truly great.

Which book do you think is truly a great example of literature? Describe the story of the book and explain why you think it is great.

## 2. The Parts of Literature

Almost every literary work includes four parts: (1) characters (2) setting (3) plot (4) theme

### (1) Characters

The characters are the people that we follow in a story. They can be real people or fictional characters made in the writer's mind. When we read a book, we learn about the characters and read about what happens in their lives. In a story there are main characters and supporting characters. The main characters are the most important. Also, there is usually a hero who is good, and a villain who is bad.

### (2) Setting

The setting is the place and time of the story. The setting can be a small village in the country or a big city like New York. The story can take place under the sea or on the moon. The time can be anywhere in the past, present, or future. Many fantasy or science fiction stories have amazing settings in worlds made in the author's mind.

### (3) Plot

Plot tells us what happens to the characters in a story. A plot usually has a beginning, middle and ending. Usually the beginning introduces the characters and the setting, the middle presents a problem or difficulty for the characters, and in the ending, the problem is solved in some way. If the characters in a book are real people, the plot will follow their lives.

### (4) Theme

Theme is the basic idea of the story or the lesson of the story. A theme may teach the readers to live a good life or a different kind of life. For example, in the famous story of the ant and grasshopper, readers learn that they must work hard in life.

1) Choose a story that you know and describe the characters, setting, plot and theme.

The name of the book : ______________________

Characters : ______________________

______________________

Plot : ______________________

______________________

Theme : ______________________

______________________

______________________

2) Write a short story that includes the four parts.

______________________

______________________

______________________

______________________

______________________

______________________

______________________

______________________

______________________

______________________

______________________